Family Day

Chelsea Kong

Printed in 2024-2025, Made in Toronto, Canada
ISBN: 978-1-998335-12-1
Library and Archives Canada

Happy Family Day

Canada celebrates it on the third
Monday of February.
Alberta, British Columbia, Ontario,
Saskatchewan celebrate.

FAMILY DAY

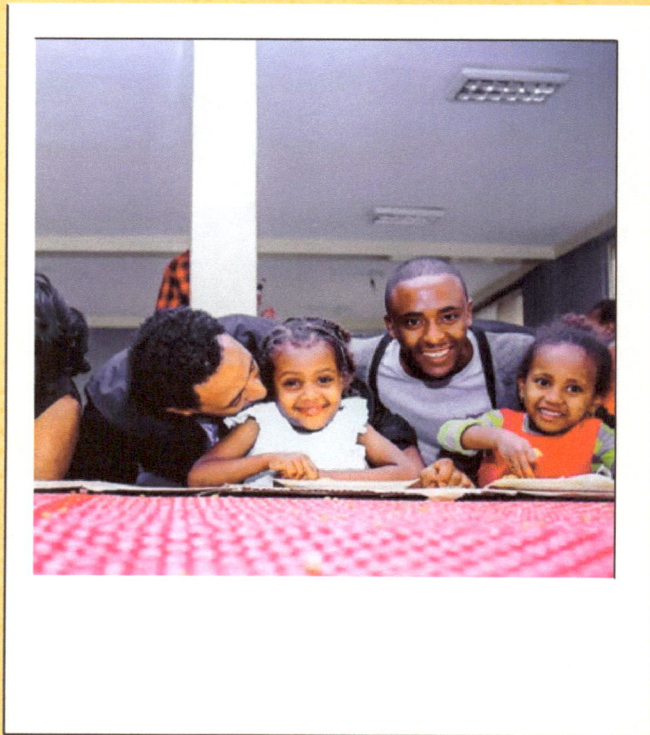

In Manitoba, its called Louis Riel Day.
Nova Scotia calls it Heritage Day.
Islander Day in Prince Edward Island.

In Yukon, they celebrate Heritage Day on the last Friday of February before the last Sunday.

Happy family

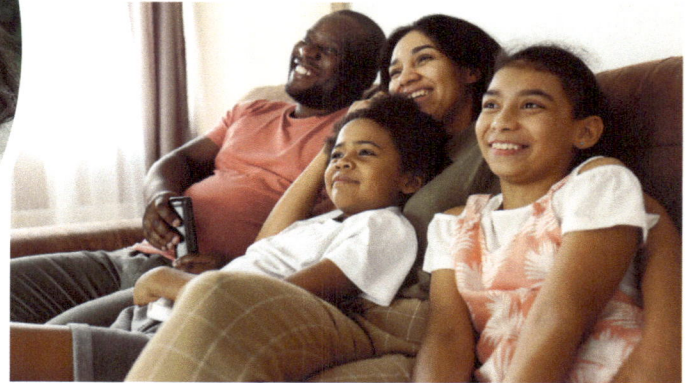

Louis Riel Day is celebrated in honor of Louis Riel, a Métis leader who fought for francophone and aboriginal rights.

To my family,

Thank you for loving me!

Heritage Day is not an official national holiday but celebrates history, architecture, and cultural heritage.

Heritage Day honours different people.
Viola Desmond who is on the $10 bill.
There are 12 people from 2015 to 2026.
They will be honoured in these years.

Family Moment

Islander Day is on the second Monday of February instead of the third. Schools and Most businesses are closed.

Corner Brook, Newfoundland calls it Civic Holiday, and it is Carnival Day. Carnival Day is on the same day.

Work Day

Quebec, Newfoundland, Labrador
don't have a holiday.
People are working on that day.

ME & YOU

It is not a federal holiday.
Not everyone celebrates it in Canada.

You should spend more time together.
Celebrate and be thankful.
Families can do fun things together.

Happy

It is a time to share our love.
Remember the good things.
You can go places together.

Show how grateful you are to your famiy. Grateful for your support!

It means a lot!

Not all families are happy.
It takes work to fix the problems.
It may not always work out.

FATHER

Do something special with
your father on this day.
Try to do something new.

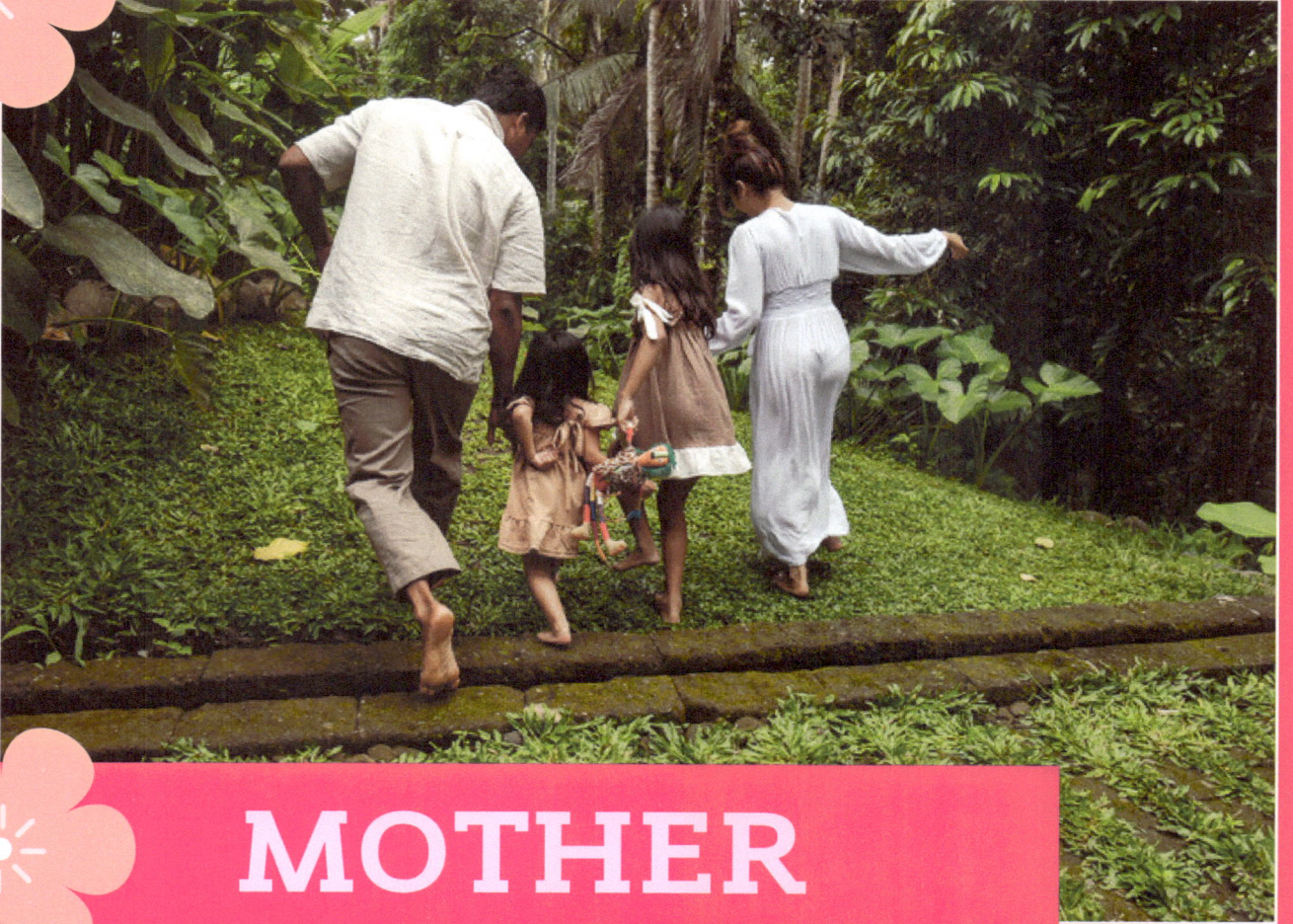

MOTHER

Do something special with your mother on this day. Take her somewhere new.

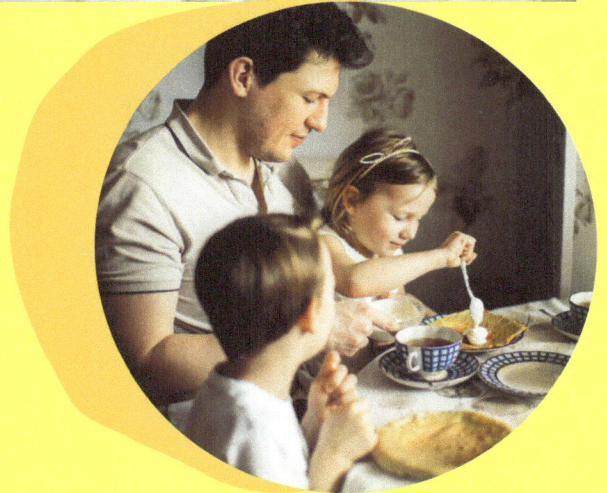

Happy families will have a good time.
They will learn to work together.
They will forgive each other.

Happy International Family Day

Families are important.
Celebrate as much as you can.

Family Day is on a different day
in the rest of the world.
Nevada celebrates after Thanksgiving.
Some celebrate on December 25 or 26.

Family Day is a public holiday in the Angola, Israel, Namibia, South Africa, Uruguay, Vanuatu, and Vietnam.

Family Day in Israel is the last day of Shevat (fifth month of the common year beginning in Tishre (or Tishri) and the 11th month of the other year in the Jewish schedule beginning in Nisan).

Family Day in Angola is December 25.

Namibia and Vanuatu celebrate
Family Day on December 26.

Uruguay celebrates on December 25.

In South Africa, Family Day
is after Easter Monday.
It is changed to Family Day.

Vietnam celebrates it on June 28th.
They give each other gifts.
They show love to each other.

infinite seascape, the village seemed compact and claustropho-
bic, its houses crowded close together in the one small corner
of the Great Blasket that faced the mainland and offered shelter.
The islanders were pragmatic people. In the years after the
evacuation they returned in *naomhóga* to strip their former
homes of doors, roof beams and slates, and anything else that
might be useful in their new lives.

At the top of the village, way above, was the two-storey house
where Peig Sayers had lived. It had been modern and strong
in 1910, but the winds had punctured the slate roof and blown
out the windows. In the seventies it was bought by a rich and
eccentric pilot from Alabama called Taylor Collings, who
visited the Great Blasket on holiday and fell in love with it.
Seized with an ambition to rebuild the village as a holiday
ranch, he called on exil
very cheaply. After all,
derelict house on an ina
bottle of brandy, or so th
than life and the people
some were sorry when h
   The next time anyone
Blasket was in the mid-e
Wall Street Journal offere
dollars. That was the sta
battle between a company
Taylor Collings's share o
– led at that time by C

Arizona and Nevada celebrate.
In Songkran, Thailand it is
celebrated on the second day.

Family Day

The first Sunday of August 1978,
Arizona celebrated the first time.

Australian Capital Territory
used to celebrate Family Day.
They changed the holiday three times.

THE LOVE IN OUR FAMILY

Make Family Day a special day.
Speak words of blessing to each other.
Pray for your family every day.

Families share love that lasts forever.
Always remember your family.
National Family Day in the USA is the
fourth Monday of September.

References

WIKIPEDIA,"FAMILY DAY (CANADA)"
WIKIPEDIA, 2024.
HTTPS://EN.WIKIPEDIA.ORG/WIKI/FAMILY_DAY_
(CANADA)

NATIONAL TODAY. "NATIONAL FAMILY DAY -
SEPTEMBER 23, 2024" NATIONAL TODAY, 2024.
HTTPS://NATIONALTODAY.COM/NATIONAL-
FAMILY-DAY/

Message from the Author

Thank you for reading this book. I hope you can leave a good review to encourage me to write more books to teach children and adults. New Brunswick and Nova Scotia will soon celebrate Family Day. USA celebrated National Family Day on Monday, September 23, 2024. The day changes, but the day of the week stays the same.

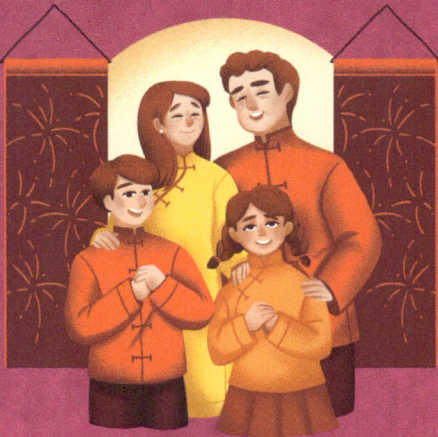

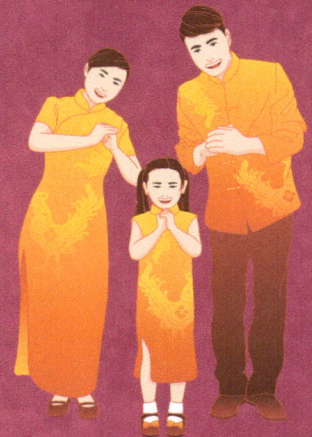

OTHER PRODUCTS

Knowing God

How to Hear God's Voice

New Life in Jesus

Loving Israel

God's Gifts/Spiritual Talents

Meeting God

Word Power

Fruit of the Spirit

The Tabernacle

Bride for Jesus

A Life of Prayer

Live Free

Who am I in Jesus

Walk in Love

God's Favor

Man of God

Woman of God

How to Use Money

God's Wisdom

Fasting

See Jerusalem and Bethany

First Fruit Offering

Feast of Trumpets

Day of Atonement

Feast of Tabernacles

Counting the Omer

Festival of Lights

Glory, Presence, and Holy Spirit

Live in God's Presence

Pentecost

See Galilee, Nazareth, and Tiberias

Hear God Speak

Knowing Jesus

Knowing Holy Spirit

A Healthy Life and Healthy Life Work Book

Smokey the Cat

Passover Unleavened Bread

Resurrection Life

The Blessing

Revival

Chelsea Learns Hebrew

Thanksgiving

Give Thanks

Jesus Birth

Loving Jesus: Bride and Groom

Proverbs 31 Woman

OTHER PRODUCTS

ABC of People in the Bible

Colours in the Bible

Breakthroughs

Open Doors

The Seven Spirits of God

Numbers in the Bible

Aglee the Eagle

An Eagle's Life

Chelsea Learns Numbers in Hebrew

ABC's of Faith

Feast of Purim

A Royal Life

Pandas

Worship

Fun in the Caribbean

Canada

Devotionals

31 Day Devotional

Inspirational/Other

Chelsea's Psalms and Poems

Your Daily Meal: Chelsea's Photo Album

Chelsea's Psalms and Poems2

Travel West Caribbean

Puzzle Books

Biblical Puzzle Book Vol 1-5

Bible Puzzles for Young Children Book 1-3

Biblical Puzzle for Children Books 1-5

Teaching Series

How to Hear God's Voice Teaching Guide & Audio Book

Relationship with God, Jesus, Holy Spirit Guide

Knowing God, Jesus, Holy Spirit Guide & Audio Book

Flowing in the Prophetic

Teaching (Non-Sale on my website)

Purim

Passover

Resurrection

More books on Amazon, Kobo, and Barnes and Noble, Smashwords, and IngramSpark.
https://chelseak532002550.wordpress.com/

More books on Amazon, Kobo, and Barnes and Noble, Smashwords, and IngramSpark.
https://www.amazon.com/author/chelseakong

Please leave a review and share with friends to help the author continue to write more books to reach more readers. Thank you so much for your support.

Review!

About
CHELSEA KONG

She is a writer, creative arts and digital media artist, skilled administration and certified PCP (Payroll Compliance Professional), and podcaster. Chelsea also served in a variety of roles, from audiovisual, photography, to assisting on the worship team, and ministry team. She also has a passion for families being united.

Chelsea has been a guest on Unity Live Radio, The Lady Tracey Show, and How to Live for Christ and is highly recommended by a Proud Christian blog. She is also a guest blogger. A few of her books have been featured in YourAuthorHub, etc. She graduated from Hotel and Restaurant Management, Digital Media Arts, Office Administration, Payroll Compliance Professional, and experience working with children. Chelsea lives in Toronto, Canada. She mainly writes children's books, stories, bridal writing, poems, lyrics for songs, words of encouragement, blessings, prayers, and jokes. The author of How to Hear the Voice of God, the Bridal Collection, Knowing God, etc. She also has her own Bible Puzzle books and other inspired products. Her podcast channel is called Chelsea K on Anchor, Spotify, and iTunes.

Please check my website to find out more:
https://chelseak532002550.wordpress.com/